A is for Adam
Growing up in Christ for Pre-readers

by Al Hiebert, PhD
illustrated by Claudia Castro Castro

19-100 Home St. N.
Steinbach, MB, Canada R5G 2G9

Library and Archives Canada Cataloguing in Publication

Hiebert, Al, 1940—, author
A is for Adam / Al Hiebert.

(Growing up in Christ)
ISBN 978-0-9868515-1-3 **(paperback)**

1. Christian life—Juvenile literature. 2. Children—Religious life—Juvenile literature. 3. English language—Alphabet—Juvenile literature. 4. Alphabet books. I. Title.

BV4571.3.H54 2015   j248.8'2   C2015-905276-9

Growing up in Christ, Inc.
19-100 Home St. N.
Steinbach, MB, Canada R5G 2G9
www.growingupinchrist.com

Illustrated by Claudia Castro Castro
Cover design by Gordan Blazevic

A is for Adam/ Al Hiebert. — 1st ed.
ISBN 978-0-9868515-1-3

To the parents

Welcome to the first book of the *Growing up in Christ* series!

This series seeks to equip Christian parents to empower their kids to grow up in Christ in a messed-up world. This book seeks to help teach your pre-school kids the alphabet and inspire them to grow up to follow Christ and to love God and His Word with all their heart, soul, mind, and strength.

This age-graduated series is designed to encourage bonding conversations between you and your kids about some significant dimensions of a faithful Christian life, including bullying and sex. This series is written from a biblical creation-fall-redemption-consummation perspective. Your kids need to see themselves and others as being created in God's image. Hence, they and all people deserve love and respect, regardless of their sometimes messed-up beliefs, behaviors, and relationships.

Nurturing kids' values is an everyday process. Note the Parents' Appendix with specific discussion suggestions. Regulate at what age you raise these questions, depending on your understanding of each child. See www.growingupinchrist.com for more suggestions on these issues. For several pages we leave it to readers to suggest discussion issues. Note also the Parents' Supplement on the last page here, including the Coloring Book edition of Book 1.

Teaching values is a daily opportunity. The Bible says: Impress them on your children. Talk about them when you sit at home and when you walk along the road, when you lie down and when you get up. (Deuteronomy 6:7 NIV)

is for Adam,
God made him whole;
Strong muscles, smart mind,
And a very kind soul.

Discuss: What is "a very kind soul"?

is for beautiful Eve
Whom God made
Perfect till she
And her man disobeyed.

Discuss: What happened when Adam and Eve disobeyed God?

 is for Christ whom
God sent here to save
All who believe.
We must not misbehave.

Discuss: How does Christ save us?

 is for Daniel
God saved in the pit
From lions!
His captors could not believe it!

 is for every brave kid
Who believes
That Jesus helps us
When others are mean.

 is for fathers
Who love their kids so,
Who teach them and show them
The way they should go.

8

 is for good times
Our family enjoys.
Mealtimes and reading
And playing with toys.

Discuss: What do you like best about your family?

is for heaven
Where loved ones have gone;
Who turned from their sin
And believed in God's son.

Discuss: Favorite memories of loved ones now gone.

 is for idols
That people adore.
Kids full of faith
Trust the Bible much more.

Discuss: What are idols?

is for Joseph
Who said, "No, No, NO!"
I want to do right,
So I'm going to GO!

Discuss: What are some wrong things others want you to do?

is for kindness
God shows us always.
We trust Him and serve
Him all of our days.

 is for love
That faithful kids show
To friends and to foes though
We're flawed as we grow.

Discuss: How can Jesus help us love our enemies (foes)?

 is for Mary
Whose child was God's son.
From heaven He came;
Soon His work here was done.

Discuss: What was Jesus' work?

 is for Nathan
God's prophet who told
King David to clean up
His mess and be bold.

*Discuss: What messes (mistakes) do we flawed kids make?
How can we clean them up?*

 is for others
In need of our aid
To hear Jesus' gospel
And plans that He made.

Discuss: How can we faithfully meet others' need?
What is Jesus' gospel?

is for precious and private
God's gifts
For girls and for boys
Who'll get married, have kids.

Discuss: What are the proper names of girls' and boys' private parts?
Why are they precious?

is for queen,
Queen Esther the brave.
She stood up to bullies
Her people to save.

Discuss: What is bullying? Why is it wrong?
How should we deal with bullies?

is for rising
To life from the dead.
Jesus did this and
Just as He said.

Discuss: Why do we believe that Jesus rose to life after He died?

**is for skin coats
God made to clothe sinners.
Adam and Eve's leaves
Were flimsy and thinner.**

Discuss: What excuses do people now use to hide their sins?

is for truth
That God gave in His Word.
Some twist it and turn it
To fit what they've heard.

Discuss: Why should we believe the Bible is true?

 is for us...and
God wants our best.
Learn how to trust Him
And He does the rest.

is for voices
We sing with delight
Of Jesus who loves us
All through the night.

Sing songs like "Jesus Loves Me," and "Jesus Loves the Little Children."

 asks "Why
Is life sometimes so tough?"
Tell bullies we love them
But enough is enough.

Discuss: What are some tough times in your life?

is eXcitement
When families have fun.
Sand castles, sliding—
We love it a ton!

Discuss: What are some of your favorite fun times in your family?

is for yesterday
We made a mistake.
We're glad some forgive us
And don't make us ache.

Discuss: What are some mistakes you have made?
Did others forgive you for these?

is for zeal that
Paul showed in God's Word
To tell Jesus' story
To those who'd not heard.

Discuss: How might you tell Jesus' story to a new friend who's not heard?

Parents' Appendix

As your kids get closer to age 5, at appropriate times you may choose to discuss selected topics listed at the bottom of some pages. Here are some suggestions to enrich those conversations.

Central ideas of *A is for Adam:*
1. Our loving, powerful, and holy God created the universe.
2. God created all people in His image.
3. All people deserve our love and respect.
4. All people need forgiveness through faith in Jesus Christ.

Think it over:
Because God created people in His image, we need to love and respect them even when their beliefs and behaviors are messed up (sinful). As Christians, we believe rude or bullying attitudes and behaviors are always wrong, as are sexual acts outside of natural marriage.

Discussions:

A and B *What is a very kind soul?*
    We are each created one person with a soul and a body. Secularists and atheists often deny the existence of our souls and moral characters. Guarding against mere materialist beliefs starts with toddlers. Teach them about their soul ("the real me" inside my body), created and deeply loved by God Himself.
    God's creating Eve must have been the pinnacle of His creation work.
    In our universe evil results from all people's sin against God. Adam and Eve started this when they disobeyed God in the Garden of Eden.

      Scriptures: Genesis 1:1-4:17; Romans 3:23; 5:12-21; 6:23; 8:18-25

C *How does Christ save us?*
    Adam and Eve became sinful (messed up) by disobeying God's command not to eat of the tree of the knowledge of good and evil. They believed the serpent instead of believing God. That's sin. We're all guilty of it. The penalty for sin is death, eternal separation from God (Romans 3:23; 5:12; 6:23).

But God in His infinite love sent Christ, His Son, to earth to save (redeem, rescue) from sin's penalty and power all who repent of (turn from) their sin and by faith accept His gift of total forgiveness. Followers of Christ seek to live for Him. Many in our culture confuse these biblical truths with distortions and lies of all sorts. Kids need to be warned of these as they grow up and hopefully embrace as their own the truths taught in the Bible. We recommend the New International Version (NIV) or the New Living Translation (NTL) for kids.

> **Scriptures**: Isaiah 64:4-5; John 1:1-3, 14, 18; 3:16-18, 36; 5:24; 10:10; 14:1-3, 6; 20:26-31; Acts 4:10, 12; 16: 31; Romans 1:21; 3:23-24; 5:8, 12, 17; 6:23; 10:13; 1 Corinthians 15:1-8; 2 Corinthians 5:21; Ephesians 2:8-10; Hebrews 10:11-12, 23; 1 John 5:11

D and E Daniel is a model of faithfulness to God in the midst of a very messed-up foreign culture in many ways similar to our own. Faithful kids need positive heroes and role models, both in Scripture and their own experiences. Dealing with bullies takes special faith in God's help and wisdom. When faced with bullies or temptation some kids like to pray, "Lord Jesus help me now" as they close their open hand one finger at a time.

> **Scriptures**: Daniel 6:1-28

F and G Family is central to God's plan for us and to the *Growing up in Christ* series. Discuss strengths and weaknesses of your family and other family options you might not identify by name (for example, where either Mom or Dad or both are missing). No family is perfect in every way. We're all messed up. There is always room for improvement and need for us to reach out in compassion and respect to everyone, especially the needy among us. Suggestions for such may generate fruitful discussions. Seek God in prayer and His Word. Discover how He would like to use your family to equip every member to know and do His will.

H Families have a heritage. Consider yours. Does it include heroes and role models your kids and you might like to imitate?

I *What are idols?*

Idols are anything we love more than God (for example, money, popularity, fun, celebrities, clothes, sports, toys, cars, TV). Use your discussion of idols to explore any negative values, ideas, or influences you think could be luring your kids away from God.

Scriptures: Exodus 20:3-4; Matthew 22:34-40

J Joseph's story invites you to explore issues such as bullying, dealing with injustices, sexual temptations, and unbiblical sexual practices. The better you understand the pressures to sin that your kids are under from others, the better you will be able to demonstrate how to cope with such pressures. Your loving responses should encourage them to come to you first with their concerns. Note safety implications of sexual touching and abuse by anyone. Only Mom or Dad or a doctor should see or touch their precious private parts for good reasons of hygiene and health. Show special compassion to any who may already have been sexually abused by anyone.

Scriptures: Genesis 37:1-36; 39: 1-23; 41:41-43; 42:6-8; 45:8; 50:20

K and L Discuss some expressions of God's kindness and love for us. Christianity is the only faith that shows God's love for sinners, including our enemies—an interesting thought. Contrary to what some secularists believe, various faiths are not all the same.

Scriptures: Jeremiah 9:23-24; 31:3-4; Matthew 5:43-48; Luke 6:34-36; 10:27; John 3:16; 5:20; 13:34-35; 14:21; 15:12; 17:27; Acts 14:16-17; Romans 5:8; 12:10, 16-21; 1 Corinthians 13:4-13; 2 Corinthians 5:14; Galatians 5:22-23; Ephesians 4:32; Colossians 3:12-13; Titus 3:3-5; 1 John 2:9-10, 15-17; 3:13-18

M Mary showed faith and obedience to God during an embarrassing and inconvenient pregnancy. Jesus' incarnation, teaching, and atonement (His great work) showed us love, self-sacrifice and obedience, though we were unworthy and messed-up sinners who were His enemies.

Scriptures: Luke 1:26-56; 2:4-20; 2 Corinthians 5:18-21; Philippians 2:5-11; Hebrews 13:11-14; 1 Peter 2:21-25

N Nathan's rebuke of King David's sin was a brave and risky example of speaking truth to one who is powerful. Sin calls for repentance. This story reminds us that God's forgiveness does not always eliminate negative consequences. We must acknowledge our sins and mistakes, seeking forgiveness and learning to make more faithful choices in the future. All humans are messed-up sinners. Thank God for His grace to forgive.

Scriptures: 2 Samuel 12:1-14, 24-25; Romans 3:23; 6:23

O Throughout your kids' growing up years, brainstorming ways to help others—and following through—can teach compassion and self-sacrifice and can become an ongoing topic of family discussion of evangelism and mercy ministries.

Scriptures: Matthew 6:2-4; 25:34-39; 28:18-20; James 1:26-27

P Pre-readers are naturally curious about how boys and girls are different. They need to learn that their private parts (those covered by swimsuits) are precious gifts from God, designed for special functions in marriage when they are ready to start their own families, whether or not they ever have babies (at this tender age we think it is inappropriate to discuss sex that does not lead to pregnancy). These precious private parts should never be touched so as to make them feel uncomfortable and should not be seen by others besides their parents or doctors. Caution them to tell you if they ever face sexual advances from anyone. Do this without scaring them unduly. Use only correct medical names (such as, "breasts," "vulva," and "vagina" for girls and "penis," "scrotum," and "testes" for boys). Those parents who prefer to use sketches of Adam and Eve that show these parts can find them at:

www.growingupinchrist.com. Book 2 (*The Kids of Messed-Up Woods*) has helpful discussions for early readers ages 5-8 in novel form. Book 3 (*God Makes Love, Truth, and Holiness Work*) adds diagrams and discussions to prepare tweens ages 8-12 for puberty. Book 4 (*Dealing with Doubts and Differences*) gives teens help on issues they face in high school and university. Book 5 (*Deciding Right from Wrong*) adds more biblical help on disputed ethical issues.

At every age kids need to learn to say no like Joseph, run away and tell Mom or Dad if anyone tries to see or touch their precious private parts. That's just as important as using seatbelts in cars, to prevent something bad from happening. Being safe does not mean being afraid, just faithful to biblical truth in a messed-up world. Some teachers of junior and senior kindergarten are promoting same-sex (two mommies or two daddies) "families" to 4- and 5-year-olds (https://www.lifesitenews.com/news/lesbian-teacher-how-i-convince-kids-to-accept-gay-marriage-starting-at-4-ye, accessed June 17, 2015). We believe that strategy is inappropriate for this tender age. However, if your child is exposed to this secular teaching you need to empower your child to deal with it with a clear conviction about the Bible's views on sex and marriage. Books 2-5 address such matters in greater detail.

Q The Queen Esther story raises the need for brave women and men to stand up against bullies and ask for help with bullying situations. Kids with safe love-bond attachments to their parents are less likely to become bullies. They are more likely to stand up to bullies bravely and seek appropriate help with them. Books 2-5 add further discussions.

Scriptures: Esther 2:1-7:10; Joshua 1:6-9

R Jesus' rising from the dead is a fact of history that many people today dismiss as myth without examining the evidences. Jesus' resurrection sets the Christian faith apart as true, quite distinct from other belief systems. Still, we need to love and respect everyone, even those who believe falsehoods (for example, the myth that all religions are equally valid or invalid).

Scriptures: John 20:1-31; 1 Corinthians 15:1-8

S God's making skin coats for Adam and Eve was likely a lesson about sin's need for atoning sacrifice. This would be made clearer many years later through Jesus' sacrifice on the cross.

> **Scriptures**: Genesis 3:15 - 4:17; 2 Corinthians 10:3-5; Ephesians 6:12-20; Hebrews 9:20-28

T The truth of the Bible is widely rejected in our messed-up world. Since Jesus trusted Scripture as God's revealed Word, should we not do the same?

> **Scriptures**: Matthew 5:17-19; 2 Timothy 3:12-17; 2 Peter 1:16-21

U Us and God wants our best is a kid's definition of the desire to grow up in Christ. Caution: Faith that "He does the rest" still needs our active faithful obedience.

V V is for voices, we sing with delight: Singing can teach kids many important Bible truths and provide them with ways to reassure themselves when they feel sad or lonely or can't sleep at night. Some songs are an easy and fun way for kids to memorize Scripture. Your kids may enjoy the two-minute "Jesus Loves Me," video at: www.youtube.com/watch?v=owx3ao42kwI or the three- verse one at: www.youtube.com/watch?v=KBALcN701NU . Also see "Jesus Loves the Little Children" and two more kids' songs at: www.youtube.com/watch?v=B_xdkk_sXgA.

> **Scriptures**: Exodus 15:1, 21; Judges 5:3; Psalm 96:1; 98:5; Acts 16:25; Colossians 3: 16

W Why is life sometimes tough? may be a question among many your kids will ask you—and should be encouraged to ask you—throughout their lives. You may not always know the answer, but you can search for it together. Moral evil (caused by people) is clearly a result of sin; non-moral evil (for example, illness, pain, and tragedies caused by natural events) is less obviously a result of the curse of sin on nature. We and the world are both messed up by sin.

Scriptures: Matthew 5:11-12; Romans 5:3-5; 8:20-24; 12:1-2; James 1:2-5

X Highlight the "eXcitement" and fun families have ... the more, the better for all. Laughter is medicine and the joy of the Lord is our strength. Enjoying the ride is allowed and encouraged.

Scriptures: Nehemiah 8:10; Psalm 35:27; 95:1; Isaiah 29:19; Philippians 4:4

Y Part of growing up in Christ is learning that we all mess up sometimes and that God's grace can deal with yesterday's mistakes, whether they're ours or someone else's. We must show grace and forgiveness to others, too, especially if they repent.

Scriptures: Matthew 6:14-15; Romans 3:23; 5:1-2, 6-11; 6:23; Ephesians 2:8-10; 4:32

Z Zeal is a special enthusiasm. Paul's zeal for evangelism is another model for us to emulate, depending on God's special gifting to us. Regarding how to tell Jesus' story to someone, you may want to use the "What if no one warned you?" tract free at: litmin.org/store/products.php?prodid=1014&do=list.

Scriptures: John 3:16-18, 36; 20:26-31; Acts 16:25-36; 17:16-34; Romans 3:23-24; 6:23; 10:1, 9-13; 2 Corinthians 2:21; 1 Timothy 2:1-7; 4:11-16; 1 John 5

Further help on this is available at www.growingupinchrist.com

Parents' Supplement

1. If you have any comments, questions, or feedback, please tell us at www.growingupinchrist.com "Contacts" page.

2. If you like this book, please tell your friends and write an honest review at your nearest Amazon site (e.g., www.Amazon.com or www.Amazon.ca, etc.) and anywhere else you think this book might be helpful to readers.

3. Also please "like" us on Facebook
   "Growing Up In Christ" (Education)

Growing up
in Christ

4. Watch for other titles in this series at

www.growingupinchrist.com:

A is for Adam Coloring Book, same rhymes and text as Book 1	*The Kids of Messed Up Woods,* a "first novel" for ages 5-8; with black and white art	*God Makes Love Truth and Holiness Work,* dialogues with tweens (ages 8-12) on puberty and related issues	*Dealing with Doubts and Differences,* essays for teens (ages 13-19) on their truth issues	*Deciding Right from Wrong,* essays for teens (ages 13-19) on their ethical issues